My First Book About
DOGS

By Kama Einhorn
Illustrated by Joe Mathieu

Random House 🏠 New York

Hello, everybodee! It is I, Professor Grover, and Elmo. Elmo would like to know more about dogs, so we invited Barkley the dog to help us read this book. Elmo, Barkley, and I, and all the doggies in this book are the same in one very important way.

Can you guess what it is?

We are all VERY FURRY.

And even though YOU are not furry like us, we still want you to read all about DOGS with us!

You want to pat the head of this doggie, right? Go ahead. Pat, pat, pat. He might also like to be scratched behind his ears. Scritch-scratch. Barkley would like it, too. Go ahead and give Barkley a pat and a scratch, too.

Now, you know that these cute and adorable doggies are just pictures in a book. And you also know you must NEVER pet a real dog you do not know. A grown-up must always introduce you first and tell you that it is okay. Okay?

Dogs can be short or tall, big or small, black or white, heavy or light.

There are hundreds of different kinds of dogs. Another word for a KIND of dog is BREED.

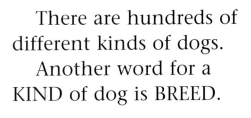

Newfoundland

Schnauzer

Yorkshire terrier

Samoyed

Shar-pei

Irish wolfhound

All dogs begin as little puppies.

When a mommy dog has babies, the group of newborn puppies is called a litter. There can be a lot of puppies in a litter.

Yorkshire terrier puppies

Newborn puppies snuggle together to stay warm. They have not even opened their eyes yet!

Litter of newborn Brittany spaniel pups

GROVE
HOMEW

Can you co
the puppies
this litter?

Barkley was a puppy once. Do you want to see his puppy pictures? Barkley was such a sweet, cuddly little puppy. Oh, he was soooo cute!

Golden retriever puppy

Dogs have fur . . .

Dog fur can be straight, curly, or wiry.

Some owne brush their hair and eve put ribbons bows in it!

Maltese

Dogs can clean themselves, and people help, too. Keeping a dog clean is called grooming.

. . . and they have tails.

Many dogs wag their tails to tell people or other dogs that they are happy or excited. Tails also help dogs keep their balance. Tails can be long or short.

English sett

ogs have four
egs with paws
nd claws.

Dogs have five
es on each paw.

Vizsla

I, Grover, have four fingers on each hand and three toes on each foot. And, of course, I have a lot of fur. But I do NOT have a tail!

ogs also have
aws on each
oe, just like
people have
toenails.

A dog uses its ears to listen . . .

There are many muscles in a dog's ear. These muscles help a dog use its ears to hear better.

A dog's ears can be little or big, pointy or floppy.

Dogs can hear sounds that people can't.

. . . and its nose to smell.

Bulldog

White wolf

dog's nose leathery nd moist.

A dog's sense of smell is much better than a person's.

Dogs sniff the ound and the air to arn what is going around them.

Basset hound

Dogs use their mouths to taste, chew, howl, bark . . .

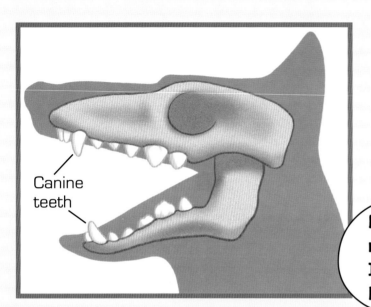

Canine teeth

A dog has 42 teeth. Dogs use their long canine teeth to tear at food. People have canine teeth, too! Can you find yours? They are the pointy ones.

Barking is a dog's way of communicating

My, Barkley, what nice teeth you have! I, Grover, do not have teeth.

. . and even to give kisses!

Different breeds have different personalities. Some dogs seem happy all the time. Some love to cuddle. Some love to hunt. Some love to run. Some love to swim. And, as with people, no two dogs are exactly the same.

Some dogs have jobs helping people. They can pull . . .

A pack of dogs pulls this hunter through the ice and snow so he can find food.

Inuit man in Greenland with dogsled team

These dogs have thick coats of fur to keep them warm.

Siberian husky

. . and protect.

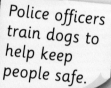

Police officers train dogs to help keep people safe.

Dalmatian

Dogs can herd . . .

Sheepdog herding flock of sheep in Scotla

Herding dogs work on farms. They keep sheep and other animals together and protect them.

. . . and they can guide.

Dogs can help people who can't hear and also those people who can't walk around easily by themselves.

eeing Eye dog

Dogs help people ho can't see. They elp them walk ound safely.

Dogs can rescue someone who is lost.

Saint Bernard

Dogs play . . . .

Many people say that of all the animals,
~~s~~ are the best to have as friends.

Wowee! Now you really know a lot about dogs. I am so proud of you! There is one last, important thing to learn, and that is: How does a person take care of a dog? Well, I, Grover, am going to tell you!

Pets need:
* Food
* Water
* Walking
* A warm place to sleep
* Brushing
* Baths
* Veterinary care
(A doctor who takes care of animals is called a veterinarian.)
* LOVE!